CARDIAC DIET NINJA AIR FRYER COOKBOOK

Lysandra Quinn

DISCLAIMER

The content within this book reflects my thoughts, experiences, and beliefs. It is meant for informational and entertainment purposes. While I have taken great care to provide accurate information, I cannot guarantee the absolute correctness or applicability of the content to every individual or situation. Please consult with relevant professionals for advice specific to your needs.

ACKNOWLEDGMENTS

I want to express my deepest gratitude to those who have supported and encouraged me on this creative journey. Your love, patience, and inspiration have been the driving force behind this book. I also thank the talented team of professionals who have contributed their skills to bring this book to life.

TABLE OF CONTENTS

INTRODUCTION

In the hushed corners of my heart, there's a story that's both personal and powerful. It's a story that I've carried with me, a story of transformation, and ultimately, a story of hope. It all began with a book, my first culinary guide, "The Slow Cooker Cardiac Diet Cooker," and how it changed not just my life but the life of the person who means the world to me - my mother.

You see, my mother has always been the epitome of strength and resilience. She's the woman who taught me that a mother's love knows no bounds. She's the one who was there for me, cheering me on, every step of the way when I decided to become a dietician. She was my inspiration, my guiding light.

But life had its twists and turns. A few years ago, my mother was diagnosed with a heart condition that sent shockwaves through our family. It was a sobering moment that shook us to our core. We were faced with the harsh reality that our matriarch, the heart of our home, was now battling a condition that demanded not just our love and support but also a complete overhaul of her lifestyle, especially her diet.

Determined to make a difference and give my mother the best chance at a healthier life, I immersed myself in the world of heart-healthy cooking. My search led me to the wonders of the slow cooker, where I discovered that delicious and wholesome meals could be created with minimal effort. The slow cooker became my ally, and its recipes filled our home with tempting aromas and flavorful dishes.

The Slow Cooker Cardiac Diet Cooker was a game-changer. It turned bland and boring heart-healthy meals into delightful feasts. I could see the change in my mother's health and her outlook on life. It wasn't just about managing her condition; it was about embracing a life filled with vitality and joy.

But life is ever evolving, and so was my quest for culinary innovation. As I scoured the culinary world for new techniques, I stumbled upon the Ninja Air Fryer. The word "Ninja" in its name piqued my interest. It sounded like something that could revolutionize the way we cooked our heart-healthy meals. So, I embarked on a journey to uncover the magic hidden within this modern kitchen wonder.

As I delved deeper into the world of Ninja Air Fryer cooking, I realized that it held a treasure trove of possibilities for creating delicious, heart-healthy dishes. The Ninja Air Fryer wasn't just a kitchen appliance; it was a gateway to a new way of life, one that would make heart-healthy eating a pleasure rather than a chore.

I began experimenting with a wide array of recipes, from Breakfast Delights that started our day with a burst of energy to Heart-Healthy Main Courses that transformed dinner into a grand culinary adventure. I tried out Sides and Salads that turned ordinary vegetables into gourmet creations, and Vegetarian and Vegan Options that proved that plant-based dishes could be both satisfying and delightful.

But it was the Desserts with a Twist that truly stole the show. I found myself whipping up mouthwatering desserts that not only satisfied our sweet cravings but also adhered to the cardiac diet principles. There were Air-Fried Banana and Walnut Oatmeal Cookies, Air-Fried Apple and Cinnamon Wonton Pockets, and even Air-Fried Chocolate-Dipped Strawberries with Almonds. These desserts weren't just delicious; they were a celebration of life, love, and good health.

It was during this culinary exploration that a transformative event occurred, one that would eventually inspire me to write this cookbook. One evening, after preparing a heart-healthy feast using the Ninja Air Fryer, my family sat down to eat. The table was adorned with dishes that looked and smelled divine. But it wasn't just about the food; it was about the laughter, the conversations, and the shared moments.

As my mother savoured every bite of the meal, her eyes sparkled with a newfound zest for life. The joy on her face was a testament to the power of food to heal, nourish, and bring people together. It was at that very moment that I knew I had to share these recipes with the world. There were countless families out there facing the same challenges, searching for ways to make heart-healthy cooking a source of joy rather than a burden.

My passion for nutrition, combined with the magic of the Ninja Air Fryer, had unlocked a new chapter in our lives. This cookbook is a culmination of that journey, a journey of discovery, transformation, and unwavering love.

In the pages that follow, you'll find a treasure trove of heart-healthy recipes that are as delicious as they are nutritious. These recipes have been crafted with love and care, inspired by my mother's journey and the countless individuals who, like her, strive to lead heart-healthy lives.

It's a cookbook filled with flavourful Breakfast Delights, satisfying Main Courses, delectable Sides and Salads, and tantalizing Desserts with a Twist. Each recipe is a testament to the idea that heart-healthy eating can be an indulgent experience, a journey of joy, and a celebration of life.

So, as you embark on this culinary adventure with me, I hope you'll discover the magic of the Ninja Air Fryer and experience the transformation it can bring to your life. Let's cook with love, Savor the Flavors, and celebrate the gift of good health. This cookbook is not just a collection of recipes; it's a story of hope, healing, and the boundless power of the heart.

Welcome to the world of "Ninja Air Fryer Magic: A Heart-Healthy Culinary Journey."

Chapter 1

About the Cardiac Diet

Maintaining a heart-healthy diet is crucial for preventing cardiovascular diseases and promoting overall well-being. The cardiac diet, often recommended by healthcare professionals, focuses on consuming foods that support heart health. One way to adhere to this dietary plan while still enjoying delicious meals is by using a Ninja Air Fryer. In this article, we will explore the benefits of the cardiac diet, how a Ninja Air Fryer can assist in preparing heart-healthy meals and provide tips for healthy cooking.

The Cardiac Diet

The cardiac diet, also known as the heart-healthy diet, is designed to reduce the risk of heart disease and manage existing cardiovascular conditions. It emphasizes the consumption of nutrient-rich, low-sodium, and low-cholesterol foods, while minimizing the intake of saturated and trans fats. Key components of the cardiac diet include:

Fruits and Vegetables: A rich source of vitamins, minerals, and fiber, fruits and vegetables help lower blood pressure and reduce the risk of heart disease.

Lean Proteins: Skinless poultry, fish, legumes, and lean cuts of meat provide necessary protein without the saturated fats found in red and processed meats.

Whole Grains: Whole grains like brown rice, quinoa, and whole wheat pasta are high in fiber and can help control cholesterol levels.

Healthy Fats: Incorporating sources of healthy fats, such as avocados, nuts, and olive oil, can improve heart health.

Low-Fat Dairy: Opt for low-fat or fat-free dairy products to reduce saturated fat intake.

The Role of the Ninja Air Fryer

The Ninja Air Fryer is a versatile kitchen appliance that uses hot air to cook food, providing a healthier alternative to traditional deep frying. Here's how it can benefit the cardiac diet:

Reduced Oil Usage: The Ninja Air Fryer requires little to no oil, allowing you to enjoy crispy foods without the excess saturated fats associated with deep frying.

Healthier Cooking Methods: It uses air circulation to cook food, eliminating the need for submerging items in oil, which can lead to a reduction in calorie and fat content.

Retains Nutrients: The air frying process retains more of the nutrients in your ingredients, especially when compared to boiling or deep frying.

Versatility: You can use the Ninja Air Fryer to prepare a wide range of heart-healthy meals, from vegetable fries to baked fish or chicken.

Tips for Healthy Cooking

When cooking heart-healthy meals with the Ninja Air Fryer, consider the following tips:

Choose the Right Ingredients: Opt for fresh, whole ingredients and lean proteins to create nutritious dishes.

Limit Salt and Sodium: Be mindful of sodium intake by using herbs, spices, and low-sodium seasoning options to flavor your food.

Use Healthy Oils Sparingly: While air frying requires minimal oil, choose heart-healthy options like olive or avocado oil when needed.

Control Portions: Pay attention to portion sizes to manage calorie intake and maintain a healthy weight.

Experiment with Recipes: Get creative with your Ninja Air Fryer, trying out new recipes that incorporate heart-healthy foods.

Chapter 2

Breakfast Delights

Air-Fried Oatmeal Pancakes

Cooking Time: 8 minutes

Serving: 2

Ingredients:

- ✓ 1 cup old-fashioned oats
- ✓ 1 ripe banana, mashed.
- ✓ 1/2 cup almond milk
- ✓ 1 tsp cinnamon
- ✓ 1/2 tsp vanilla extract
- ✓ 1/4 tsp baking powder

Instructions:

1. In a blender, combine all ingredients and blend until smooth.
2. Preheat the Ninja Air Fryer to 350°F (175°C).
3. Pour pancake batter onto the air fryer tray.
4. Air fry for 8 minutes, flipping halfway through.

Nutritional Information (per serving):

Approximately 250 calories, 5g protein, 4g fat, 50g carbohydrates.

Air-Fried Veggie Omelet

Cooking Time: 10 minutes

Serving: 2

Ingredients:

- ✓ 4 large eggs
- ✓ 1/2 cup diced bell peppers.
- ✓ 1/2 cup diced onions.
- ✓ 1/2 cup diced tomatoes.
- ✓ Salt and pepper to taste

Instructions:

1. Whisk eggs in a bowl and season with salt and pepper.
2. Preheat the Ninja Air Fryer to 350°F (175°C).
3. Pour the egg mixture into the air fryer tray.
4. Sprinkle vegetables on top.
5. Air fry for 10 minutes or until the omelet is set.

Nutritional Information (per serving):

Approximately 160 calories, 12g protein, 10g fat, 8g carbohydrates.

Air-Fried Banana Nut Muffins

Cooking Time: 15 minutes

Serving: 4

Ingredients:

- ✓ 2 ripe bananas, mashed.
- ✓ 1 cup whole wheat flour
- ✓ 1/4 cup chopped walnuts.
- ✓ 1/4 cup honey
- ✓ 1/4 cup plain Greek yogurt.
- ✓ 1 tsp baking powder

Instructions:

1. In a bowl, mix mashed bananas, flour, walnuts, honey, yogurt, and baking powder.
2. Preheat the Ninja Air Fryer to 350°F (175°C).
3. Divide the batter into muffin cups.
4. Air fry for 15 minutes or until a toothpick comes out clean.

Nutritional Information (per serving):

Approximately 200 calories, 5g protein, 6g fat, 35g carbohydrates.

Air-Fried Breakfast Burritos

Cooking Time: 10 minutes

Serving: 2

Ingredients:

- ✓ 4 whole wheat tortillas
- ✓ 4 large eggs, scrambled.
- ✓ 1/2 cup diced bell peppers.
- ✓ 1/2 cup diced onions.
- ✓ 1/4 cup shredded low-fat cheddar cheese.
- ✓ Salt and pepper to taste

Instructions:

1. Place tortillas on a clean surface.
2. Fill each tortilla with scrambled eggs, peppers, onions, and cheese.
3. Preheat the Ninja Air Fryer to 350°F (175°C).
4. Place the burritos in the air fryer.
5. Air fry for 10 minutes or until golden brown.

Nutritional Information (per serving):

Approximately 320 calories, 18g protein, 12g fat, 30g carbohydrates.

Air-Fried Blueberry Banana Bread

Cooking Time: 25 minutes

Serving: 8

Ingredients:

- ✓ 2 ripe bananas, mashed.
- ✓ 1/2 cup plain Greek yogurt.
- ✓ 1/4 cup honey
- ✓ 2 large eggs
- ✓ 2 cups whole wheat flour
- ✓ 1 tsp baking soda
- ✓ 1 cup fresh blueberries

Instructions:

1. Preheat the Ninja Air Fryer to 325°F (160°C).
2. In a bowl, mix mashed bananas, yogurt, honey, and eggs.
3. Stir in flour and baking soda until well combined.
4. Gently fold in blueberries.
5. Pour the batter into a greased air fryer-safe pan.
6. Air fry for 25 minutes or until a toothpick comes out clean.

Nutritional Information (per serving):

Approximately 180 calories, 6g protein, 2.5g fat, 35g carbohydrates.

Air-Fried Quinoa Breakfast Bowl

Cooking Time: 15 minutes

Serving: 2

Ingredients:

- ✓ 1 cup cooked quinoa
- ✓ 1/2 cup mixed berries
- ✓ 1/4 cup low-fat Greek yogurt
- ✓ 2 tbsp honey
- ✓ 1/4 cup chopped almonds.

Instructions:

1. Preheat the Ninja Air Fryer to 325°F (160°C).
2. In a bowl, layer quinoa, berries, yogurt, honey, and almonds.
3. Air fry for 15 minutes until warm.

Nutritional Information (per serving):

Approximately 290 calories, 10g protein, 8g fat, 45g carbohydrates.

Air-Fried Sweet Potato Hash

Cooking Time: 12 minutes

Serving: 4

Ingredients:

- ✓ 2 sweet potatoes, diced.
- ✓ 1/2 cup diced onions.
- ✓ 1/2 cup diced bell peppers.
- ✓ 1 tsp olive oil
- ✓ 1/2 tsp paprika
- ✓ Salt and pepper to taste

Instructions:

1. Toss sweet potatoes, onions, and bell peppers with olive oil, paprika, salt, and pepper.
2. Preheat the Ninja Air Fryer to 375°F (190°C).
3. Air fry the hash for 12 minutes, shaking the basket halfway through.

Nutritional Information (per serving):

Approximately 110 calories, 2g protein, 2g fat, 20g carbohydrates.

Air-Fried Egg and Vegetable Breakfast Sandwich

Cooking Time: 10 minutes

Serving: 2

Ingredients:

- ✓ 4 whole wheat English muffins
- ✓ 4 large eggs
- ✓ 1/2 cup diced tomatoes.
- ✓ 1/2 cup spinach leaves
- ✓ 1/4 cup low-fat cheddar cheese
- ✓ Salt and pepper to taste

Instructions:

1. Split English muffins in half and lightly toast them.
2. In a bowl, beat eggs and season with salt and pepper.
3. Preheat the Ninja Air Fryer to 325°F (160°C).
4. Pour the beaten eggs into the air fryer tray.
5. Layer with tomatoes, spinach, and cheese.
6. Air fry for 10 minutes.

Nutritional Information (per serving):

Approximately 290 calories, 16g protein, 9g fat, 35g carbohydrates.

Air-Fried Avocado Toast

Cooking Time: 6 minutes

Serving: 2

Ingredients:

- ✓ 2 slices whole wheat bread
- ✓ 1 ripe avocado, mashed.
- ✓ 1 tsp lemon juice
- ✓ 1/4 tsp red pepper flakes
- ✓ Salt and pepper to taste

Instructions:

1. Mix mashed avocado with lemon juice, red pepper flakes, salt, and pepper.
2. Toast the whole wheat bread.
3. Preheat the Ninja Air Fryer to 325°F (160°C).
4. Spread the avocado mixture on the toast.
5. Air fry for 6 minutes until the edges are crispy.

Nutritional Information (per serving):

Approximately 200 calories, 4g protein, 10g fat, 25g carbohydrates.

Air-Fried Greek Yogurt Parfait

Cooking Time: 5 minutes

Serving: 2

Ingredients:

- ✓ 1 cup low-fat Greek yogurt
- ✓ 1/2 cup mixed berries
- ✓ 1/4 cup granola
- ✓ 1 tbsp honey

Instructions:

1. In a bowl or glass, layer Greek yogurt, berries, granola, and drizzle with honey.
2. Preheat the Ninja Air Fryer to 325°F (160°C).
3. Air fry for 5 minutes to slightly warm and enhance the flavors.

Nutritional Information (per serving):

Approximately 250 calories, 15g protein, 6g fat, 35g carbohydrates.

Chapter 3

Appetizers and Snacks

Air-Fried Sweet Potato Fries

Cooking Time: 15 minutes

Serving: 4

Ingredients:

- ✓ 2 sweet potatoes, cut into thin strips.
- ✓ 1 tsp olive oil
- ✓ 1/2 tsp paprika
- ✓ Salt and pepper to taste

Instructions:

1. Toss sweet potato strips with olive oil, paprika, salt, and pepper.
2. Preheat the Ninja Air Fryer to 375°F (190°C).
3. Air fry the sweet potato fries for 15 minutes, shaking the basket occasionally.

Nutritional Information (per serving):

Approximately 120 calories, 2g protein, 2g fat, 25g carbohydrates.

Air-Fried Zucchini Chips

Cooking Time: 10 minutes

Serving: 2

Ingredients:

- ✓ 2 zucchinis, sliced into thin rounds.
- ✓ 1 tsp olive oil
- ✓ 1/4 cup grated Parmesan cheese
- ✓ 1/2 tsp garlic powder
- ✓ Salt and pepper to taste

Instructions:

1. Toss zucchini slices with olive oil, Parmesan, garlic powder, salt, and pepper.
2. Preheat the Ninja Air Fryer to 375°F (190°C).
3. Air fry the zucchini chips for 10 minutes, flipping once.

Nutritional Information (per serving):

Approximately 90 calories, 5g protein, 3g fat, 10g carbohydrates.

Air-Fried Stuffed Mushrooms

Cooking Time: 12 minutes

Serving: 4

Ingredients:

- ✓ 12 large mushrooms, stems removed and chopped.
- ✓ 1/4 cup diced onions.
- ✓ 1/4 cup diced bell peppers.
- ✓ 1/4 cup whole wheat breadcrumbs
- ✓ 2 tbsp grated Parmesan cheese
- ✓ 1 tsp olive oil

Instructions:

1. In a bowl, combine mushroom stems, onions, bell peppers, breadcrumbs, Parmesan, and olive oil.
2. Preheat the Ninja Air Fryer to 350°F (175°C).
3. Stuff mushroom caps with the mixture.
4. Air fry the stuffed mushrooms for 12 minutes.

Nutritional Information (per serving):

Approximately 70 calories, 4g protein, 3g fat, 8g carbohydrates.

Air-Fried Spinach and Feta Phyllo Triangles

Cooking Time: 10 minutes

Serving: 4

Ingredients:

- ✓ 4 sheets of phyllo dough, cut into squares.
- ✓ 1 cup chopped spinach.
- ✓ 1/4 cup crumbled feta cheese
- ✓ 1/2 tsp olive oil
- ✓ Salt and pepper to taste

Instructions:

1. In a bowl, mix spinach, feta, olive oil, salt, and pepper.
2. Place a spoonful of the mixture in the center of each phyllo square.
3. Fold into triangles and seal the edges.
4. Preheat the Ninja Air Fryer to 375°F (190°C).
5. Air fry the phyllo triangles for 10 minutes.

Nutritional Information (per serving):

Approximately 90 calories, 4g protein, 4g fat, 10g carbohydrates.

Air-Fried Hummus-Stuffed Mushrooms

Cooking Time: 10 minutes

Serving: 4

Ingredients:

- ✓ 12 large mushrooms, stems removed and reserved.
- ✓ 1/2 cup low-sodium hummus
- ✓ 1/4 cup diced red bell pepper.
- ✓ 1/4 cup chopped fresh parsley.
- ✓ Salt and pepper to taste

Instructions:

1. Finely chop mushroom stems and combine with hummus, bell pepper, parsley, salt, and pepper.
2. Preheat the Ninja Air Fryer to 350°F (175°C).
3. Stuff mushroom caps with the hummus mixture.
4. Air fry the stuffed mushrooms for 10 minutes.

Nutritional Information (per serving):

Approximately 70 calories, 3g protein, 3g fat, 8g carbohydrates.

Air-Fried Cauliflower Bites

Cooking Time: 12 minutes

Serving: 4

Ingredients:

- ✓ 1 small head of cauliflower, cut into florets.
- ✓ 1/4 cup whole wheat flour
- ✓ 1/4 cup water
- ✓ 1 tsp garlic powder
- ✓ 1/2 tsp paprika
- ✓ Salt and pepper to taste

Instructions:

1. In a bowl, whisk together flour, water, garlic powder, paprika, salt, and pepper.
2. Dip cauliflower florets into the batter, allowing excess to drip off.
3. Preheat the Ninja Air Fryer to 375°F (190°C).
4. Air fry the cauliflower bites for 12 minutes, shaking the basket occasionally.

Nutritional Information (per serving):

Approximately 80 calories, 3g protein, 1g fat, 15g carbohydrates.

Air-Fried Guacamole-Stuffed Jalapeños

Cooking Time: 10 minutes

Serving: 4

Ingredients:

- ✓ 8 large jalapeño peppers halved and seeded.
- ✓ 1 avocado, mashed.
- ✓ 1/4 cup diced tomatoes.
- ✓ 1/4 cup diced onions.
- ✓ 1/4 cup chopped cilantro.
- ✓ Salt and pepper to taste

Instructions:

1. In a bowl, combine mashed avocado, tomatoes, onions, cilantro, salt, and pepper.
2. Stuff jalapeño halves with guacamole mixture.
3. Preheat the Ninja Air Fryer to 375°F (190°C).
4. Air fry the jalapeños for 10 minutes.

Nutritional Information (per serving):

Approximately 90 calories, 2g protein, 7g fat, 7g carbohydrates.

Air-Fried Quinoa-Stuffed Bell Peppers

Cooking Time: 12 minutes

Serving: 4

Ingredients:

- ✓ 4 bell peppers, tops removed, and seeds removed.
- ✓ 1 cup cooked quinoa
- ✓ 1/2 cup black beans, drained and rinsed.
- ✓ 1/2 cup corn kernels
- ✓ 1/4 cup salsa
- ✓ 1/4 cup shredded low-fat cheddar cheese.
- ✓ Salt and pepper to taste

Instructions:

1. In a bowl, mix quinoa, black beans, corn, salsa, cheese, salt, and pepper.
2. Stuff the peppers with the mixture.
3. Preheat the Ninja Air Fryer to 350°F (175°C).
4. Air fry the stuffed peppers for 12 minutes.

Nutritional Information (per serving):

Approximately 250 calories, 10g protein, 2g fat, 50g carbohydrates.

Air-Fried Cucumber Dill Bites

Cooking Time: 6 minutes

Serving: 2

Ingredients:

- ✓ 1 cucumber, sliced into rounds.
- ✓ 1/4 cup low-fat Greek yogurt
- ✓ 1 tbsp fresh dill, chopped.
- ✓ 1 tsp lemon juice
- ✓ Salt and pepper to taste

Instructions:

1. In a bowl, mix Greek yogurt, dill, lemon juice, salt, and pepper.
2. Top each cucumber slice with the yogurt mixture.
3. Preheat the Ninja Air Fryer to 325°F (160°C).
4. Air fry the cucumber bites for 6 minutes.

Nutritional Information (per serving):

Approximately 50 calories, 3g protein, 1g fat, 8g carbohydrates.

Air-Fried Edamame

Cooking Time: 8 minutes

Serving: 4

Ingredients:

- ✓ 2 cups frozen edamame, thawed.
- ✓ 1 tsp olive oil
- ✓ 1/2 tsp sea salt
- ✓ 1/4 tsp garlic powder

Instructions:

1. Toss edamame with olive oil, sea salt, and garlic powder.
2. Preheat the Ninja Air Fryer to 375°F (190°C).
3. Air fry the edamame for 8 minutes, shaking the basket occasionally.

Nutritional Information (per serving):

Approximately 90 calories, 7g protein, 3g fat, 8g carbohydrates.

Chapter 4

Heart-Healthy Main Courses

Lemon Herb Air-Fried Salmon

Cooking Time: 12 minutes

Serving: 2

Ingredients:

- ✓ 2 salmon fillets
- ✓ 1 lemon, sliced.
- ✓ 1 tsp olive oil
- ✓ 1 tsp dried herbs (rosemary, thyme, oregano)
- ✓ Salt and pepper to taste

Instructions:

1. Preheat the Ninja Air Fryer to 375°F (190°C).
2. Brush salmon with olive oil, season with herbs, salt, and pepper.
3. Place lemon slices on top of the fillets.
4. Air fry for 12 minutes or until the salmon flakes easily.

Nutritional Information (per serving):

Approximately 250 calories, 30g protein, 10g fat, 5g carbohydrates.

Air-Fried Herb-Crusted Chicken Breast

Cooking Time: 18 minutes

Serving: 2

Ingredients:

- ✓ 2 boneless, skinless chicken breasts
- ✓ 1/2 cup whole wheat breadcrumbs
- ✓ 1 tsp dried Italian herbs
- ✓ 1/4 cup grated Parmesan cheese
- ✓ Salt and pepper to taste

Instructions:

1. Combine breadcrumbs, herbs, Parmesan, salt, and pepper.
2. Coat chicken breasts with the breadcrumb mixture.
3. Preheat the Ninja Air Fryer to 375°F (190°C).
4. Air fry the chicken for 18 minutes, turning once.

Nutritional Information (per serving):

Approximately 280 calories, 35g protein, 5g fat, 20g carbohydrates.

Air-Fried Mediterranean Chicken Kebabs

Cooking Time: 15 minutes

Serving: 4

Ingredients:

- ✓ 1 lb boneless, skinless chicken breast, cut into chunks.
- ✓ 1 red bell pepper, cut into chunks.
- ✓ 1 red onion, cut into chunks.
- ✓ 2 tbsp olive oil
- ✓ 1 tsp dried oregano
- ✓ Salt and pepper to taste

Instructions:

1. In a bowl, marinate chicken, bell pepper, and onion with olive oil, oregano, salt, and pepper.
2. Thread the marinated ingredients onto skewers.
3. Preheat the Ninja Air Fryer to 375°F (190°C).
4. Air fry the kebabs for 15 minutes, turning once.

Nutritional Information (per serving):

Approximately 220 calories, 25g protein, 10g fat, 10g carbohydrates.

Air-Fried Quinoa and Black Bean Stuffed Peppers

Cooking Time: 15 minutes

Serving: 4

Ingredients:

- ✓ 4 bell peppers, tops removed, and seeds removed.
- ✓ 1 cup cooked quinoa
- ✓ 1 can (15 oz) black beans, drained and rinsed.
- ✓ 1 cup diced tomatoes.
- ✓ 1/2 cup corn kernels
- ✓ 1/4 cup chopped fresh cilantro.
- ✓ 1 tsp chili powder
- ✓ Salt and pepper to taste

Instructions:

1. In a bowl, combine quinoa, black beans, tomatoes, corn, cilantro, chili powder, salt, and pepper.
2. Stuff the peppers with the mixture.
3. Preheat the Ninja Air Fryer to 350°F (175°C).
4. Air fry the stuffed peppers for 15 minutes.

Nutritional Information (per serving):

Approximately 260 calories, 10g protein, 2.5g fat, 50g carbohydrates.

Air-Fried Shrimp and Vegetable Stir-Fry

Cooking Time: 10 minutes

Serving: 2

Ingredients:

- ✓ 1/2 lb large shrimp, peeled and deveined.
- ✓ 2 cups mixed vegetables (broccoli, bell peppers, snap peas)
- ✓ 2 tbsp low-sodium soy sauce
- ✓ 1 tbsp honey
- ✓ 1 tsp minced garlic
- ✓ 1 tsp ginger

Instructions:

1. In a bowl, whisk together soy sauce, honey, garlic, and ginger.
2. Toss shrimp and mixed vegetables in the sauce.
3. Preheat the Ninja Air Fryer to 375°F (190°C).
4. Air fry the shrimp and vegetable stir-fry for 10 minutes, shaking the basket halfway through.

Nutritional Information (per serving):

Approximately 220 calories, 25g protein, 2g fat, 30g carbohydrates.

Air-Fried Herb-Crusted Tofu

Cooking Time: 12 minutes

Serving: 4

Ingredients:

- ✓ 1 block extra-firm tofu, sliced into rectangles.
- ✓ 1/2 cup whole wheat breadcrumbs
- ✓ 1 tsp dried Italian herbs
- ✓ 1/4 cup grated Parmesan cheese
- ✓ Salt and pepper to taste

Instructions:

1. Combine breadcrumbs, herbs, Parmesan, salt, and pepper.
2. Coat tofu slices with the breadcrumb mixture.
3. Preheat the Ninja Air Fryer to 375°F (190°C).
4. Air fry the tofu for 12 minutes, turning once.

Nutritional Information (per serving):

Approximately 200 calories, 15g protein, 8g fat, 20g carbohydrates.

Air-Fried Vegetable and Chickpea Curry

Cooking Time: 20 minutes

Serving: 4

Ingredients:

- ✓ 2 cups mixed vegetables (cauliflower, carrots, peas)
- ✓ 1 can (15 oz) chickpeas, drained and rinsed.
- ✓ 1 can (15 oz) diced tomatoes.
- ✓ 1/2 cup low-sodium vegetable broth
- ✓ 2 tbsp curry powder
- ✓ Salt and pepper to taste

Instructions:

1. In a bowl, mix mixed vegetables, chickpeas, diced tomatoes, vegetable broth, curry powder, salt, and pepper.
2. Preheat the Ninja Air Fryer to 375°F (190°C).
3. Air fry the vegetable and chickpea curry for 20 minutes, stirring occasionally.

Nutritional Information (per serving):

Approximately 220 calories, 10g protein, 2g fat, 40g carbohydrates.

Air-Fried Turkey Meatballs with Marinara

Cooking Time: 15 minutes

Serving: 4

Ingredients:

- ✓ 1 lb lean ground turkey
- ✓ 1/4 cup whole wheat breadcrumbs
- ✓ 1/4 cup grated Parmesan cheese
- ✓ 1/4 cup chopped fresh parsley.
- ✓ 1/4 cup diced onions.
- ✓ 1 egg
- ✓ Salt and pepper to taste
- ✓ 1 cup low-sodium marinara sauce

Instructions:

1. Combine all meatball ingredients in a bowl and form into meatballs.
2. Preheat the Ninja Air Fryer to 375°F (190°C).
3. Air fry the turkey meatballs for 15 minutes, turning once.
4. Serve with warm marinara sauce.

Nutritional Information (per serving):

Approximately 220 calories, 25g protein, 10g fat, 10g carbohydrates.

Air-Fried Lemon-Herb Tilapia

Cooking Time: 10 minutes

Serving: 2

Ingredients:

- ✓ 2 tilapia fillets
- ✓ 1 lemon, sliced.
- ✓ 1 tsp olive oil
- ✓ 1 tsp dried herbs (rosemary, thyme, oregano)
- ✓ Salt and pepper to taste

Instructions:

1. Preheat the Ninja Air Fryer to 375°F (190°C).
2. Brush tilapia fillets with olive oil, season with herbs, salt, and pepper.
3. Place lemon slices on top of the fillets.
4. Air fry for 10 minutes or until the tilapia flakes easily.

Nutritional Information (per serving):

Approximately 200 calories, 25g protein, 6g fat, 5g carbohydrates.

Chapter 5

Sides and Salads

Air-Fried Brussels Sprouts with Balsamic Glaze

Cooking Time: 12 minutes

Serving: 4

Ingredients:

- ✓ 1 lb Brussels sprouts, trimmed and halved.
- ✓ 1 tbsp olive oil
- ✓ 2 tbsp balsamic vinegar
- ✓ Salt and pepper to taste

Instructions:

1. Toss Brussels sprouts with olive oil, balsamic vinegar, salt, and pepper.
2. Preheat the Ninja Air Fryer to 375°F (190°C).
3. Air fry the Brussels sprouts for 12 minutes, shaking the basket occasionally.
4. Drizzle with extra balsamic glaze before serving.

Nutritional Information (per serving):

Approximately 90 calories, 3g protein, 4g fat, 12g carbohydrates.

Air-Fried Asparagus with Lemon

Cooking Time: 10 minutes

Serving: 4

Ingredients:

- ✓ 1 bunch asparagus, trimmed.
- ✓ 1 tbsp olive oil
- ✓ Zest and juice of 1 lemon
- ✓ Salt and pepper to taste

Instructions:

1. Toss asparagus with olive oil, lemon zest, lemon juice, salt, and pepper.
2. Preheat the Ninja Air Fryer to 375°F (190°C).
3. Air fry the asparagus for 10 minutes, shaking the basket occasionally.

Nutritional Information (per serving):

Approximately 60 calories, 2g protein, 4g fat, 5g carbohydrates.

Air-Fried Sweet Potato Wedges

Cooking Time: 15 minutes

Serving: 4

Ingredients:

- ✓ 2 large, sweet potatoes, cut into wedges.
- ✓ 1 tbsp olive oil
- ✓ 1 tsp paprika
- ✓ Salt and pepper to taste

Instructions:

1. Toss sweet potato wedges with olive oil, paprika, salt, and pepper.
2. Preheat the Ninja Air Fryer to 375°F (190°C).
3. Air fry the sweet potato wedges for 15 minutes, shaking the basket occasionally.

Nutritional Information (per serving):

Approximately 110 calories, 2g protein, 3g fat, 20g carbohydrates.

Air-Fried Quinoa Salad with Roasted Vegetables

Cooking Time: 20 minutes

Serving: 4

Ingredients:

- ✓ 1 cup cooked quinoa
- ✓ 2 cups mixed roasted vegetables (bell peppers, zucchini, carrots)
- ✓ 1/4 cup chopped fresh parsley
- ✓ 2 tbsp olive oil
- ✓ 2 tbsp lemon juice
- ✓ Salt and pepper to taste

Instructions:

1. In a bowl, combine quinoa, roasted vegetables, parsley, olive oil, lemon juice, salt, and pepper.
2. Preheat the Ninja Air Fryer to 375°F (190°C).
3. Air fry the quinoa salad for 5 minutes to warm.

Nutritional Information (per serving):

Approximately 160 calories, 4g protein, 7g fat, 20g carbohydrates.

Air-Fried Garlic Parmesan Green Beans

Cooking Time: 10 minutes

Serving: 4

Ingredients:

- ✓ 1 lb green beans, trimmed.
- ✓ 1 tbsp olive oil
- ✓ 2 cloves garlic, minced.
- ✓ 2 tbsp grated Parmesan cheese
- ✓ Salt and pepper to taste

Instructions:

1. Toss green beans with olive oil, garlic, Parmesan, salt, and pepper.
2. Preheat the Ninja Air Fryer to 375°F (190°C).
3. Air fry the green beans for 10 minutes, shaking the basket occasionally.

Nutritional Information (per serving):

Approximately 80 calories, 2g protein, 4g fat, 10g carbohydrates.

Air-Fried Cucumber Tomato Salad

Cooking Time: 5 minutes

Serving: 4

Ingredients:

- ✓ 2 cucumbers, sliced.
- ✓ 2 tomatoes, diced.
- ✓ 1/4 cup red onion thinly sliced.
- ✓ 2 tbsp fresh dill, chopped.
- ✓ 2 tbsp red wine vinegar
- ✓ 1 tbsp olive oil
- ✓ Salt and pepper to taste

Instructions:

1. In a bowl, combine cucumbers, tomatoes, red onion, dill, red wine vinegar, olive oil, salt, and pepper.
2. Preheat the Ninja Air Fryer to 325°F (160°C).
3. Air fry the cucumber tomato salad for 5 minutes to slightly warm and meld the flavors.

Nutritional Information (per serving):

Approximately 60 calories, 1g protein, 3g fat, 8g carbohydrates.

Air-Fried Stuffed Avocado

Cooking Time: 10 minutes

Serving: 2

Ingredients:

- ✓ 2 ripe avocados halved and pitted.
- ✓ 1/2 cup cooked quinoa
- ✓ 1/2 cup black beans, drained and rinsed.
- ✓ 1/4 cup diced tomatoes.
- ✓ 2 tbsp chopped fresh cilantro.
- ✓ 1 tbsp lime juice
- ✓ Salt and pepper to taste

Instructions:

1. In a bowl, mix quinoa, black beans, tomatoes, cilantro, lime juice, salt, and pepper.
2. Stuff avocado halves with the mixture.
3. Preheat the Ninja Air Fryer to 350°F (175°C).
4. Air fry the stuffed avocados for 10 minutes.

Nutritional Information (per serving):

Approximately 280 calories, 7g protein, 15g fat, 30g carbohydrates.

Air-Fried Kale Chips

Cooking Time: 5 minutes

Serving: 2

Ingredients:

- ✓ 4 cups fresh kale leaves, torn into bite-sized pieces.
- ✓ 1 tbsp olive oil
- ✓ 1/2 tsp garlic powder
- ✓ Salt and pepper to taste

Instructions:

1. Toss kale leaves with olive oil, garlic powder, salt, and pepper.
2. Preheat the Ninja Air Fryer to 325°F (160°C).
3. Air fry the kale chips for 5 minutes until crispy.

Nutritional Information (per serving): Approximately 50 calories, 2g protein, 3g fat, 5g carbohydrates.

Air-Fried Mediterranean Quinoa Salad

Cooking Time: 15 minutes

Serving: 4

Ingredients:

- ✓ 2 cups cooked quinoa.
- ✓ 1/2 cup diced cucumber.
- ✓ 1/2 cup diced tomatoes.
- ✓ 1/4 cup chopped fresh parsley.
- ✓ 1/4 cup crumbled feta cheese
- ✓ 2 tbsp olive oil
- ✓ 2 tbsp lemon juice
- ✓ Salt and pepper to taste

Instructions:

1. In a bowl, combine quinoa, cucumber, tomatoes, parsley, feta, olive oil, lemon juice, salt, and pepper.
2. Preheat the Ninja Air Fryer to 350°F (175°C).
3. Air fry the quinoa salad for 5 minutes to warm.

Nutritional Information (per serving):

Approximately 180 calories, 6g protein, 10g fat, 15g carbohydrates.

Air-Fried Beet and Orange Salad

Cooking Time: 8 minutes

Serving: 4

Ingredients:

- ✓ 4 medium beets peeled and diced.
- ✓ 2 oranges peeled and segmented.
- ✓ 1/4 cup chopped fresh mint.
- ✓ 2 tbsp balsamic vinegar
- ✓ 1 tbsp olive oil
- ✓ Salt and pepper to taste

Instructions:

1. Toss beets with olive oil, balsamic vinegar, salt, and pepper.
2. Preheat the Ninja Air Fryer to 375°F (190°C).
3. Air fry the beets for 8 minutes, until tender.
4. Let the beets cool and mix with oranges and fresh mint.

Nutritional Information (per serving): Approximately 110 calories, 2g protein, 3g fat, 20g carbohydrates.

Chapter 6

Vegetarian and Vegan Options

Air-Fried Tofu and Vegetable Stir-Fry (Vegan)

Cooking Time: 15 minutes

Serving: 2

Ingredients:

- ✓ 1 block extra-firm tofu, cubed.
- ✓ 2 cups mixed vegetables (broccoli, bell peppers, snap peas)
- ✓ 2 tbsp low-sodium soy sauce
- ✓ 1 tbsp maple syrup
- ✓ 1 tsp minced garlic
- ✓ 1 tsp ginger

Instructions:

1. Toss tofu and mixed vegetables with soy sauce, maple syrup, garlic, and ginger.
2. Preheat the Ninja Air Fryer to 375°F (190°C).
3. Air fry the tofu and vegetable stir-fry for 15 minutes, shaking the basket occasionally.

Nutritional Information (per serving):

Approximately 250 calories, 15g protein, 8g fat, 30g carbohydrates.

Air-Fried Stuffed Bell Peppers with Lentils (Vegan)

Cooking Time: 15 minutes

Serving: 4

Ingredients:

- ✓ 4 bell peppers, tops removed, and seeds removed.
- ✓ 1 cup cooked green or brown lentils.
- ✓ 1 cup diced tomatoes.
- ✓ 1/2 cup diced onions.
- ✓ 1/4 cup chopped fresh parsley.
- ✓ 1 tsp cumin
- ✓ Salt and pepper to taste

Instructions:

1. In a bowl, mix lentils, tomatoes, onions, parsley, cumin, salt, and pepper.
2. Stuff the peppers with the mixture.
3. Preheat the Ninja Air Fryer to 350°F (175°C).
4. Air fry the stuffed peppers for 15 minutes.

Nutritional Information (per serving):

Approximately 180 calories, 8g protein, 1g fat, 35g carbohydrates.

Air-Fried Vegetable Spring Rolls (Vegan)

Cooking Time: 10 minutes

Serving: 4

Ingredients:

- ✓ 8 spring roll wrappers
- ✓ 2 cups shredded cabbage.
- ✓ 1 cup shredded carrots
- ✓ 1/2 cup sliced bell peppers.
- ✓ 1/4 cup chopped fresh cilantro.
- ✓ 1/4 cup low-sodium soy sauce
- ✓ 1 tsp sesame oil

Instructions:

1. Combine shredded cabbage, carrots, bell peppers, cilantro, soy sauce, and sesame oil.
2. Assemble the spring rolls with the mixture.
3. Preheat the Ninja Air Fryer to 375°F (190°C).
4. Air fry the spring rolls for 10 minutes, turning once.

Nutritional Information (per serving):

Approximately 110 calories, 3g protein, 1g fat, 20g carbohydrates.

Air-Fried Falafel (Vegan)

Cooking Time: 12 minutes

Serving: 4

Ingredients:

- ✓ 1 can (15 oz) chickpeas, drained and rinsed.
- ✓ 1/4 cup diced onions.
- ✓ 1/4 cup chopped fresh parsley.
- ✓ 1 tsp ground cumin
- ✓ 1 tsp ground coriander
- ✓ Salt and pepper to taste

Instructions:

1. In a food processor, combine chickpeas, onions, parsley, cumin, coriander, salt, and pepper.
2. Form the mixture into small patties.
3. Preheat the Ninja Air Fryer to 375°F (190°C).
4. Air fry the falafel for 12 minutes, turning once.

Nutritional Information (per serving): Approximately 150 calories, 7g protein, 3g fat, 25g carbohydrates.

Air-Fried Stuffed Mushrooms with Spinach and Vegan Cheese (Vegan)

Cooking Time: 12 minutes

Serving: 4

Ingredients:

- ✓ 12 large mushrooms, stems removed and chopped.
- ✓ 1/2 cup chopped spinach.
- ✓ 1/4 cup vegan cream cheese
- ✓ 1/4 cup vegan mozzarella cheese
- ✓ 1/4 cup diced onions.
- ✓ 1 tsp olive oil

Instructions:

1. In a bowl, combine mushroom stems, spinach, vegan cream cheese, vegan mozzarella, onions, and olive oil.
2. Stuff mushroom caps with the mixture.
3. Preheat the Ninja Air Fryer to 350°F (175°C).
4. Air fry the stuffed mushrooms for 12 minutes.

Nutritional Information (per serving):

Approximately 90 calories, 2g protein, 4g fat, 10g carbohydrates.

Air-Fried Eggplant Parmesan (Vegan)

Cooking Time: 15 minutes

Serving: 4

Ingredients:

- ✓ 1 large eggplant, sliced into rounds.
- ✓ 1 cup whole wheat breadcrumbs
- ✓ 1/2 cup marinara sauce (vegan)
- ✓ 1/4 cup vegan mozzarella cheese
- ✓ 1 tsp dried basil
- ✓ Salt and pepper to taste

Instructions:

1. Coat eggplant slices with whole wheat breadcrumbs, basil, salt, and pepper.
2. Preheat the Ninja Air Fryer to 375°F (190°C).
3. Air fry the eggplant slices for 15 minutes, turning once.
4. Top with marinara sauce and vegan mozzarella before serving.

Nutritional Information (per serving):

Approximately 140 calories, 4g protein, 3g fat, 25g carbohydrates.

Air-Fried Sweet Potato and Chickpea Salad (Vegan)

Cooking Time: 10 minutes

Serving: 4

Ingredients:

- ✓ 2 cups cubed sweet potatoes.
- ✓ 1 can (15 oz) chickpeas, drained and rinsed.
- ✓ 1/4 cup diced red onion.
- ✓ 2 tbsp olive oil
- ✓ 1 tsp cumin
- ✓ Salt and pepper to taste

Instructions:

1. Toss sweet potatoes, chickpeas, red onion, olive oil, cumin, salt, and pepper.
2. Preheat the Ninja Air Fryer to 375°F (190°C).
3. Air fry the sweet potato and chickpea salad for 10 minutes, shaking the basket occasionally.

Nutritional Information (per serving): Approximately 180 calories, 6g protein, 6g fat, 25g carbohydrates.

Air-Fried Zucchini Fritters (Vegan)

Cooking Time: 10 minutes

Serving: 4

Ingredients:

- ✓ 2 cups grated zucchini.
- ✓ 1/4 cup chickpea flour
- ✓ 1/4 cup chopped scallions.
- ✓ 1 tsp ground cumin
- ✓ Salt and pepper to taste

Instructions:

1. In a bowl, combine grated zucchini, chickpea flour, scallions, cumin, salt, and pepper.
2. Form the mixture into small patties.
3. Preheat the Ninja Air Fryer to 375°F (190°C).
4. Air fry the zucchini fritters for 10 minutes, turning once.

Nutritional Information (per serving):

Approximately 90 calories, 3g protein, 2g fat, 15g carbohydrates.

Air-Fried Stuffed Portobello Mushrooms with Quinoa and Spinach (Vegan)

Cooking Time: 15 minutes

Serving: 2

Ingredients:

- ✓ 2 large portobello mushrooms, stems removed and chopped.
- ✓ 1 cup cooked quinoa
- ✓ 1 cup chopped spinach.
- ✓ 1/4 cup diced tomatoes.
- ✓ 2 tbsp balsamic vinegar
- ✓ 1 tbsp olive oil
- ✓ Salt and pepper to taste

Instructions:

1. In a bowl, mix mushroom stems, quinoa, spinach, tomatoes, balsamic vinegar, olive oil, salt, and pepper.
2. Stuff portobello mushrooms with the mixture.
3. Preheat the Ninja Air Fryer to 350°F (175°C).
4. Air fry the stuffed mushrooms for 15 minutes.

Nutritional Information (per serving): Approximately 240 calories, 6g protein, 6g fat, 40g carbohydrates.

Air-Fried Stuffed Peppers with Quinoa and Black Beans (Vegan)

Cooking Time: 15 minutes

Serving: 4

Ingredients:

- ✓ 4 bell peppers, tops removed, and seeds removed.
- ✓ 1 cup cooked quinoa
- ✓ 1 can (15 oz) black beans, drained and rinsed.
- ✓ 1 cup diced tomatoes.
- ✓ 1/2 cup corn kernels
- ✓ 1/4 cup chopped fresh cilantro.
- ✓ 1 tsp chili powder
- ✓ Salt and pepper to taste

Instructions:

1. In a bowl, combine quinoa, black beans, tomatoes, corn, cilantro, chili powder, salt, and pepper.
2. Stuff the peppers with the mixture.
3. Preheat the Ninja Air Fryer to 350°F (175°C).
4. Air fry the stuffed peppers for 15 minutes.

Nutritional Information (per serving):

Approximately 260 calories, 10g protein, 2.5g fat, 50g carbohydrates.

Chapter 7

Low-Sodium and Flavorful Sauces

Low-Sodium Marinara Sauce

Cooking Time: 15 minutes

Serving: 4

Ingredients:

- ✓ 1 can (28 oz) crushed tomatoes (no salt added)
- ✓ 1/4 cup diced onions.
- ✓ 2 cloves garlic, minced.
- ✓ 1 tsp olive oil
- ✓ 1 tsp dried basil
- ✓ 1/2 tsp dried oregano

Instructions:

1. In a saucepan, heat olive oil and sauté onions and garlic until softened.
2. Add crushed tomatoes, basil, and oregano.
3. Simmer for 15 minutes, stirring occasionally.

Nutritional Information (per serving):

Approximately 40 calories, 1g protein, 1g fat, 8g carbohydrates.

Low-Sodium Pesto Sauce

Cooking Time: 5 minutes

Serving: 4

Ingredients:

- ✓ 2 cups fresh basil leaves
- ✓ 1/4 cup pine nuts, toasted.
- ✓ 2 cloves garlic
- ✓ 2 tbsp grated Parmesan cheese
- ✓ 2 tbsp lemon juice
- ✓ 2 tbsp olive oil
- ✓ Salt and pepper to taste

Instructions:

1. In a food processor, blend basil, pine nuts, garlic, Parmesan, lemon juice, and olive oil until smooth.
2. Season with salt and pepper.

Nutritional Information (per serving): Approximately 100 calories, 3g protein, 9g fat, 4g carbohydrates.

Low-Sodium Teriyaki Sauce

Cooking Time: 10 minutes

Serving: 4

Ingredients:

- ✓ 1/2 cup low-sodium soy sauce
- ✓ 1/4 cup water
- ✓ 2 tbsp honey
- ✓ 1 tbsp grated ginger
- ✓ 2 cloves garlic, minced.

Instructions:

1. In a saucepan, combine soy sauce, water, honey, ginger, and garlic.
2. Bring to a simmer and cook for 10 minutes, stirring occasionally.

Nutritional Information (per serving):

Approximately 50 calories, 2g protein, 0g fat, 12g carbohydrates.

Low-Sodium Cilantro-Lime Sauce

Cooking Time: 5 minutes

Serving: 4

Ingredients:

- ✓ 1 cup fresh cilantro leaves
- ✓ 1/4 cup plain Greek yogurt (low sodium)
- ✓ 2 cloves garlic
- ✓ 2 tbsp lime juice
- ✓ 1 tsp olive oil
- ✓ Salt and pepper to taste

Instructions:

1. In a blender, combine cilantro, yogurt, garlic, lime juice, and olive oil until smooth.
2. Season with salt and pepper.

Nutritional Information (per serving):

Approximately 30 calories, 2g protein, 1g fat, 4g carbohydrates.

Low-Sodium Lemon-Dill Sauce

Cooking Time: 5 minutes

Serving: 4

Ingredients:

- ✓ 1/2 cup low-sodium plain yogurt
- ✓ 2 tbsp fresh dill, chopped.
- ✓ 1 tbsp lemon juice
- ✓ 1 clove garlic, minced.
- ✓ Salt and pepper to taste

Instructions:

1. In a bowl, mix yogurt, dill, lemon juice, and garlic.
2. Season with salt and pepper.

Nutritional Information (per serving): Approximately 25 calories, 2g protein, 0g fat, 4g carbohydrates.

Low-Sodium Barbecue Sauce

Cooking Time: 15 minutes

Serving: 4

Ingredients:

- ✓ 1/2 cup tomato sauce (no salt added)
- ✓ 1/4 cup apple cider vinegar
- ✓ 2 tbsp honey
- ✓ 1 tbsp Worcestershire sauce (low sodium)
- ✓ 1 tsp smoked paprika.
- ✓ 1/2 tsp garlic powder

Instructions:

1. In a saucepan, combine tomato sauce, apple cider vinegar, honey, Worcestershire sauce, paprika, and garlic powder.
2. Simmer for 15 minutes, stirring occasionally.

Nutritional Information (per serving):

Approximately 50 calories, 0g protein, 0g fat, 14g carbohydrates.

Low-Sodium Tzatziki Sauce

Cooking Time: 5 minutes

Serving: 4

Ingredients:

- ✓ 1 cup low-sodium Greek yogurt
- ✓ 1/2 cucumber grated and drained.
- ✓ 2 cloves garlic, minced.
- ✓ 1 tbsp lemon juice
- ✓ 1 tsp fresh dill, chopped.
- ✓ Salt and pepper to taste

Instructions:

1. In a bowl, combine Greek yogurt, grated cucumber, garlic, lemon juice, and dill.
2. Season with salt and pepper.

Nutritional Information (per serving):

Approximately 40 calories, 4g protein, 0g fat, 6g carbohydrates.

Low-Sodium Salsa Verde

Cooking Time: 10 minutes

Serving: 4

Ingredients:

- ✓ 1 cup fresh tomatillos husked and chopped.
- ✓ 1/4 cup diced onions.
- ✓ 1/4 cup fresh cilantro
- ✓ 1 clove garlic
- ✓ 1 tsp lime juice
- ✓ 1/2 tsp olive oil
- ✓ Salt and pepper to taste

Instructions:

1. In a blender, combine tomatillos, onions, cilantro, garlic, lime juice, and olive oil until smooth.
2. Season with salt and pepper.

Nutritional Information (per serving):

Approximately 25 calories, 1g protein, 1g fat, 5g carbohydrates.

Low-Sodium Lemon-Caper Sauce

Cooking Time: 10 minutes

Serving: 4

Ingredients:

- ✓ 1/2 cup low-sodium vegetable broth
- ✓ 2 tbsp capers
- ✓ 1 tbsp lemon juice
- ✓ 1 tsp olive oil
- ✓ 1 tsp fresh thyme

Instructions:

1. In a saucepan, combine vegetable broth, capers, lemon juice, olive oil, and thyme.
2. Simmer for 10 minutes, stirring occasionally.

Nutritional Information (per serving):

Approximately 15 calories, 0g protein, 1g fat, 2g carbohydrates.

Low-Sodium Roasted Red Pepper Sauce

Cooking Time: 10 minutes

Serving: 4

Ingredients:

- ✓ 2 roasted red peppers, peeled, and diced.
- ✓ 1/4 cup low-sodium vegetable broth
- ✓ 2 cloves garlic
- ✓ 1 tsp olive oil
- ✓ 1/2 tsp smoked paprika.
- ✓ Salt and pepper to taste

Instructions:

1. In a blender, combine roasted red peppers, vegetable broth, garlic, olive oil, smoked paprika, salt, and pepper until smooth.
2. Heat the sauce in a saucepan for 10 minutes, stirring occasionally.

Nutritional Information (per serving):

Approximately 20 calories, 1g protein, 1g fat, 4g carbohydrates.

Chapter 8

Desserts with a Twist

Air-Fried Banana and Walnut Oatmeal Cookies

Cooking Time: 10 minutes

Serving: 4

Ingredients:

- ✓ 2 ripe bananas, mashed.
- ✓ 1 cup old-fashioned oats
- ✓ 1/4 cup chopped walnuts.
- ✓ 2 tbsp honey
- ✓ 1 tsp ground cinnamon

Instructions:

1. In a bowl, combine mashed bananas, oats, walnuts, honey, and cinnamon.
2. Drop spoonfuls of the mixture onto the air fryer tray.
3. Preheat the Ninja Air Fryer to 350°F (175°C) and air fry the cookies for 10 minutes.

Nutritional Information (per serving):

Approximately 160 calories, 3g protein, 5g fat, 26g carbohydrates.

Air-Fried Apple and Cinnamon Wonton Pockets

Cooking Time: 12 minutes

Serving: 4

Ingredients:

- ✓ 2 apples, diced.
- ✓ 1 tsp cinnamon
- ✓ 1/4 cup honey
- ✓ 8 wonton wrappers

Instructions:

1. In a bowl, combine diced apples, cinnamon, and honey.
2. Place a spoonful of the apple mixture in the center of each wonton wrapper.
3. Fold the wrappers to form pockets.
4. Preheat the Ninja Air Fryer to 350°F (175°C) and air fry the pockets for 12 minutes.

Nutritional Information (per serving):

Approximately 160 calories, 2g protein, 1g fat, 38g carbohydrates.

Air-Fried Dark Chocolate and Raspberry Stuffed Dates

Cooking Time: 6 minutes

Serving: 4

Ingredients:

- ✓ 8 Medjool dates, pitted.
- ✓ 8 dark chocolate chips
- ✓ 8 fresh raspberries

Instructions:

1. Stuff each date with one dark chocolate chip and one raspberry.
2. Preheat the Ninja Air Fryer to 350°F (175°C) and air fry the stuffed dates for 6 minutes.

Nutritional Information (per serving):

Approximately 80 calories, 1g protein, 1g fat, 18g carbohydrates.

Air-Fried Pineapple and Coconut Spring Rolls

Cooking Time: 8 minutes

Serving: 4

Ingredients:

- ✓ 1 cup diced pineapple.
- ✓ 1/4 cup shredded coconut
- ✓ 8 spring roll wrappers

Instructions:

1. Combine diced pineapple and shredded coconut.
2. Place a spoonful of the pineapple-coconut mixture in the center of each spring roll wrapper.
3. Fold the wrappers to form spring rolls.
4. Preheat the Ninja Air Fryer to 375°F (190°C) and air fry the spring rolls for 8 minutes.

Nutritional Information (per serving):

Approximately 140 calories, 2g protein, 4g fat, 24g carbohydrates.

Air-Fried Pumpkin and Almond Butter Bites

Cooking Time: 10 minutes

Serving: 4

Ingredients:

- ✓ 1/2 cup canned pumpkin puree.
- ✓ 1/4 cup almond butter
- ✓ 1/4 cup honey
- ✓ 1 tsp pumpkin pie spice
- ✓ 1 cup old-fashioned oats

Instructions:

1. In a bowl, mix pumpkin puree, almond butter, honey, pumpkin pie spice, and oats.
2. Shape the mixture into bite-sized balls.
3. Preheat the Ninja Air Fryer to 350°F (175°C) and air fry the bites for 10 minutes.

Nutritional Information (per serving):

Approximately 150 calories, 4g protein, 7g fat, 20g carbohydrates.

Air-Fried Pear and Cinnamon Empanadas

Cooking Time: 12 minutes

Serving: 4

Ingredients:

- ✓ 2 pears, diced.
- ✓ 1 tsp cinnamon
- ✓ 1/4 cup honey
- ✓ 8 empanada wrappers

Instructions:

1. Toss diced pears with cinnamon and honey.
2. Place a spoonful of the pear mixture in the center of each empanada wrapper.
3. Fold the wrappers to form empanadas.
4. Preheat the Ninja Air Fryer to 350°F (175°C) and air fry the empanadas for 12 minutes.

Nutritional Information (per serving):

Approximately 180 calories, 2g protein, 1g fat, 42g carbohydrates.

Air-Fried Blueberry and Lemon Cheesecake Spring Rolls

Cooking Time: 10 minutes

Serving: 4

Ingredients:

- ✓ 1/2 cup low-fat cream cheese
- ✓ 1/4 cup fresh blueberries
- ✓ Zest and juice of 1 lemon
- ✓ 4 spring roll wrappers

Instructions:

1. In a bowl, mix cream cheese, blueberries, lemon zest, and lemon juice.
2. Place a spoonful of the cream cheese mixture in the center of each spring roll wrapper.
3. Fold the wrappers to form spring rolls.
4. Preheat the Ninja Air Fryer to 350°F (175°C) and air fry the spring rolls for 10 minutes.

Nutritional Information (per serving):

Approximately 120 calories, 3g protein, 2g fat, 23g carbohydrates.

Air-Fried Carrot and Raisin Cake Bites

Cooking Time: 8 minutes

Serving: 4

Ingredients:

- ✓ 1 cup shredded carrots
- ✓ 1/4 cup raisins
- ✓ 1/4 cup honey
- ✓ 1 tsp ground cinnamon
- ✓ 1 cup almond flour

Instructions:

1. In a bowl, combine shredded carrots, raisins, honey, cinnamon, and almond flour.
2. Shape the mixture into bite-sized cakes.
3. Preheat the Ninja Air Fryer to 350°F (175°C) and air fry the cake bites for 8 minutes.

Nutritional Information (per serving):

Approximately 140 calories, 4g protein, 7g fat, 17g carbohydrates.

Air-Fried Chocolate-Dipped Strawberries with Almonds

Cooking Time: 6 minutes

Serving: 4

Ingredients:

- ✓ 8 large strawberries
- ✓ 2 oz dark chocolate, melted (70% cocoa or higher)
- ✓ 2 tbsp chopped almonds

Instructions:

1. Dip each strawberry in melted dark chocolate and sprinkle with chopped almonds.
2. Place the strawberries on the air fryer tray.
3. Preheat the Ninja Air Fryer to 350°F (175°C) and air fry the strawberries for 6 minutes.

Nutritional Information (per serving):

Approximately 80 calories, 1g protein, 4g fat, 11g carbohydrates.

Air-Fried Avocado and Dark Chocolate Egg Rolls

Cooking Time: 10 minutes

Serving: 4

Ingredients:

- ✓ 2 avocados, sliced.
- ✓ 4 oz dark chocolate (70% cocoa or higher), melted.
- ✓ 4 egg roll wrappers

Instructions:

1. Place a slice of avocado and a piece of dark chocolate in the center of each egg roll wrapper.
2. Fold the wrappers to form egg rolls.
3. Preheat the Ninja Air Fryer to 350°F (175°C) and air fry the egg rolls for 10 minutes.

Nutritional Information (per serving):

Approximately 130 calories, 2g protein, 7g fat, 17g carbohydrates.

Chapter 9

28-Day Meal Plan

Day	Breakfast	Lunch	Dinner	Snack
1	Banana Walnut Oatmeal Muffins	Quinoa Salad with Lemon-Dijon Dressing	Air-Fried Lemon Garlic Shrimp with Broccoli	Air-Fried Cilantro-Lime Chickpeas
2	Veggie Omelet	Air-Fried Stuffed Bell Peppers	Air-Fried Falafel with Tzatziki Sauce	Air-Fried Stuffed Mushrooms with Spinach
3	Greek Yogurt Parfait	Air-Fried Zucchini Fritters	Air-Fried Eggplant Parmesan with Salad	Air-Fried Sweet Potato and Chickpea Salad
4	Air-Fried Stuffed Mushrooms	Air-Fried Eggplant Parmesan Salad	Air-Fried Stuffed Bell Peppers	Air-Fried Stuffed Peppers with Quinoa
5	Blueberry Pancakes	Air-Fried Sweet Potato and Chickpea Salad	Air-Fried Stuffed Mushrooms with Spinach	Air-Fried Tofu and Vegetable Stir-Fry

6	Air-Fried Sweet Potato and Chickpea Salad	Air-Fried Tofu and Vegetable Stir-Fry	Air-Fried Stuffed Peppers with Quinoa	Air-Fried Vegetable Spring Rolls
7	Air-Fried Stuffed Bell Peppers	Air-Fried Vegetable Spring Rolls	Air-Fried Stuffed Mushrooms with Spinach	Air-Fried Falafel with Tzatziki Sauce
8	Greek Yogurt Parfait	Air-Fried Falafel with Tzatziki Sauce	Air-Fried Stuffed Bell Peppers	Air-Fried Eggplant Parmesan with Salad
9	Air-Fried Eggplant Parmesan Salad	Air-Fried Stuffed Mushrooms with Spinach	Air-Fried Eggplant Parmesan with Salad	Air-Fried Stuffed Mushrooms with Spinach
10	Air-Fried Stuffed Mushrooms	Air-Fried Eggplant Parmesan Salad	Air-Fried Stuffed Bell Peppers	Air-Fried Falafel with Tzatziki Sauce
11	Banana Walnut Oatmeal Muffins	Quinoa Salad with Lemon-Dijon Dressing	Air-Fried Lemon Garlic Shrimp with Broccoli	Air-Fried Cilantro-Lime Chickpeas
12	Veggie Omelette	Air-Fried Stuffed Bell Peppers	Air-Fried Falafel with	Air-Fried Stuffed

			Tzatziki Sauce	Mushrooms with Spinach
13	Greek Yogurt Parfait	Air-Fried Zucchini Fritters	Air-Fried Eggplant Parmesan with Salad	Air-Fried Sweet Potato and Chickpea Salad
14	Air-Fried Stuffed Mushrooms	Air-Fried Eggplant Parmesan Salad	Air-Fried Stuffed Bell Peppers	Air-Fried Stuffed Peppers with Quinoa
15	Blueberry Pancakes	Air-Fried Sweet Potato and Chickpea Salad	Air-Fried Stuffed Mushrooms with Spinach	Air-Fried Tofu and Vegetable Stir-Fry
16	Air-Fried Sweet Potato and Chickpea Salad	Air-Fried Tofu and Vegetable Stir-Fry	Air-Fried Stuffed Peppers with Quinoa	Air-Fried Vegetable Spring Rolls
17	Air-Fried Stuffed Bell Peppers	Air-Fried Vegetable Spring Rolls	Air-Fried Stuffed Mushrooms with Spinach	Air-Fried Falafel with Tzatziki Sauce
18	Greek Yogurt Parfait	Air-Fried Falafel with Tzatziki Sauce	Air-Fried Stuffed Bell Peppers	Air-Fried Eggplant Parmesan with Salad

19	Air-Fried Eggplant Parmesan Salad	Air-Fried Stuffed Mushrooms with Spinach	Air-Fried Eggplant Parmesan with Salad	Air-Fried Stuffed Mushrooms with Spinach
20	Air-Fried Stuffed Mushrooms	Air-Fried Eggplant Parmesan Salad	Air-Fried Stuffed Bell Peppers	Air-Fried Falafel with Tzatziki Sauce
21	Banana Walnut Oatmeal Muffins	Quinoa Salad with Lemon-Dijon Dressing	Air-Fried Lemon Garlic Shrimp with Broccoli	Air-Fried Cilantro-Lime Chickpeas
22	Veggie Omelette	Air-Fried Stuffed Bell Peppers	Air-Fried Falafel with Tzatziki Sauce	Air-Fried Stuffed Mushrooms with Spinach
23	Greek Yogurt Parfait	Air-Fried Zucchini Fritters	Air-Fried Eggplant Parmesan with Salad	Air-Fried Sweet Potato and Chickpea Salad
24	Air-Fried Stuffed Mushrooms	Air-Fried Eggplant Parmesan Salad	Air-Fried Stuffed Bell Peppers	Air-Fried Stuffed Peppers with Quinoa
25	Blueberry Pancakes	Air-Fried Sweet Potato and Chickpea Salad	Air-Fried Stuffed	Air-Fried Tofu and

			Mushrooms with Spinach	Vegetable Stir-Fry
26	Air-Fried Sweet Potato and Chickpea Salad	Air-Fried Tofu and Vegetable Stir-Fry	Air-Fried Stuffed Peppers with Quinoa	Air-Fried Vegetable Spring Rolls
27	Air-Fried Stuffed Bell Peppers	Air-Fried Vegetable Spring Rolls	Air-Fried Stuffed Mushrooms with Spinach	Air-Fried Falafel with Tzatziki Sauce
28	Greek Yogurt Parfait	Air-Fried Falafel with Tzatziki Sauce	Air-Fried Stuffed Bell Peppers	Air-Fried Eggplant Parmesan with Salad

CONCLUSION

In closing, as we turn the final pages of "Ninja Air Fryer Magic: A Heart-Healthy Culinary Journey," I want you to carry with you the warmth of love, the promise of good health, and the joy of culinary discovery. This cookbook is more than just a collection of recipes; it's a testament to the enduring power of the heart.

Our journey together has been a labor of love, inspired by my mother's resilience and the countless others who face the challenge of heart conditions. It's a journey that has shown us that heart-healthy eating can be an art, a celebration, and a profound act of self-care.

As a dietician, I've seen firsthand the impact that food has on our lives. It's not just fuel for our bodies; it's a source of nourishment for our souls. It's the thread that weaves through our most cherished memories, from family gatherings around the dinner table to intimate moments shared over a delicious meal.

Through the pages of this cookbook, I've endeavored to share that same sense of joy, love, and togetherness with you. I've offered you a glimpse into a world where heart-healthy cooking isn't a sacrifice; it's a celebration. It's a celebration of the love we have for ourselves and for those we care about.

I hope you'll take these recipes to heart, and that they become a part of your own culinary journey. May they bring warmth to your kitchen, smiles to your loved ones' faces, and nourishment to your heart.

It is my sincerest wish that this cookbook becomes a cherished companion on your path to a heart-healthy lifestyle. May it be a source of inspiration, a reminder of the beauty of good health, and a testament to the incredible power we hold to shape our destiny through our choices.

But above all, may it serve as a reminder that love, joy, and togetherness are at the heart of every meal we share. In the end, it is the love we put into our cooking, the laughter we share at the table, and the memories we create together that make every meal truly extraordinary.

Thank you for allowing me to be a part of your culinary journey. It's been an honor and a privilege to share this heartfelt journey with you. As you embark on your own path to heart-healthy living, may you savor every moment, celebrate every flavor, and treasure every beat of your healthy heart.

With love and good health.

BONUS: MEAL PLANNER JOURAL

CARDIAC DIET MEAL JOURNAL PLANNER

Weekly

WEEK _____   MONTH _____

MONDAY
BREAKFAST
LUNCH
SNACK
DINNER

TUESDAY
BREAKFAST
LUNCH
SNACK
DINNER

WEDNESDAY
BREAKFAST
LUNCH
SNACK
DINNER

THURSDAY
BREAKFAST
LUNCH
SNACK
DINNER

FRIDAY
BREAKFAST
LUNCH
SNACK
DINNER

SATURDAY
BREAKFAST
LUNCH
SNACK
DINNER

SUNDAY
BREAKFAST
LUNCH
SNACK
DINNER

SHOPPING LIST
- ○ _____
- ○ _____
- ○ _____
- ○ _____
- ○ _____
- ○ _____
- ○ _____

NOTE

CARDIAC DIET MEAL JOURNAL PLANNER

WEEK _____   MONTH _____

MONDAY
BREAKFAST
LUNCH
SNACK
DINNER

TUESDAY
BREAKFAST
LUNCH
SNACK
DINNER

WEDNESDAY
BREAKFAST
LUNCH
SNACK
DINNER

THURSDAY
BREAKFAST
LUNCH
SNACK
DINNER

FRIDAY
BREAKFAST
LUNCH
SNACK
DINNER

SATURDAY
BREAKFAST
LUNCH
SNACK
DINNER

SUNDAY
BREAKFAST
LUNCH
SNACK
DINNER

SHOPPING LIST
- ○ _____
- ○ _____
- ○ _____
- ○ _____
- ○ _____
- ○ _____
- ○ _____

NOTE

CARDIAC DIET MEAL JOURNAL PLANNER

 Weekly

WEEK _____   MONTH _____

MONDAY
BREAKFAST
LUNCH
SNACK
DINNER

TUESDAY
BREAKFAST
LUNCH
SNACK
DINNER

WEDNESDAY
BREAKFAST
LUNCH
SNACK
DINNER

THURSDAY
BREAKFAST
LUNCH
SNACK
DINNER

FRIDAY
BREAKFAST
LUNCH
SNACK
DINNER

SATURDAY
BREAKFAST
LUNCH
SNACK
DINNER

SUNDAY
BREAKFAST
LUNCH
SNACK
DINNER

SHOPPING LIST
- ○ _____
- ○ _____
- ○ _____
- ○ _____
- ○ _____
- ○ _____
- ○ _____

NOTE

CARDIAC DIET MEAL JOURNAL PLANNER

WEEK _____   **MONTH** _____

MONDAY
BREAKFAST
LUNCH
SNACK
DINNER

TUESDAY
BREAKFAST
LUNCH
SNACK
DINNER

WEDNESDAY
BREAKFAST
LUNCH
SNACK
DINNER

THURSDAY
BREAKFAST
LUNCH
SNACK
DINNER

FRIDAY
BREAKFAST
LUNCH
SNACK
DINNER

SATURDAY
BREAKFAST
LUNCH
SNACK
DINNER

SUNDAY
BREAKFAST
LUNCH
SNACK
DINNER

SHOPPING LIST
- ○ _____
- ○ _____
- ○ _____
- ○ _____
- ○ _____
- ○ _____
- ○ _____

NOTE

CARDIAC DIET MEAL JOURNAL PLANNER

WEEK _____   MONTH _____

MONDAY

BREAKFAST
LUNCH
SNACK
DINNER

TUESDAY

BREAKFAST
LUNCH
SNACK
DINNER

WEDNESDAY

BREAKFAST
LUNCH
SNACK
DINNER

THURSDAY

BREAKFAST
LUNCH
SNACK
DINNER

FRIDAY

BREAKFAST
LUNCH
SNACK
DINNER

SATURDAY

BREAKFAST
LUNCH
SNACK
DINNER

SUNDAY

BREAKFAST
LUNCH
SNACK
DINNER

SHOPPING LIST

- ○ _____
- ○ _____
- ○ _____
- ○ _____
- ○ _____
- ○ _____
- ○ _____

NOTE

CARDIAC DIET MEAL JOURNAL PLANNER

WEEK _____   MONTH _____

MONDAY
BREAKFAST
LUNCH
SNACK
DINNER

TUESDAY
BREAKFAST
LUNCH
SNACK
DINNER

WEDNESDAY
BREAKFAST
LUNCH
SNACK
DINNER

THURSDAY
BREAKFAST
LUNCH
SNACK
DINNER

FRIDAY
BREAKFAST
LUNCH
SNACK
DINNER

SATURDAY
BREAKFAST
LUNCH
SNACK
DINNER

SUNDAY
BREAKFAST
LUNCH
SNACK
DINNER

SHOPPING LIST
- ⭘ _____
- ⭘ _____
- ⭘ _____
- ⭘ _____
- ⭘ _____
- ⭘ _____
- ⭘ _____

NOTE

CARDIAC DIET MEAL JOURNAL PLANNER

WEEK _____   MONTH _____

MONDAY
BREAKFAST
LUNCH
SNACK
DINNER

TUESDAY
BREAKFAST
LUNCH
SNACK
DINNER

WEDNESDAY
BREAKFAST
LUNCH
SNACK
DINNER

THURSDAY
BREAKFAST
LUNCH
SNACK
DINNER

FRIDAY
BREAKFAST
LUNCH
SNACK
DINNER

SATURDAY
BREAKFAST
LUNCH
SNACK
DINNER

SUNDAY
BREAKFAST
LUNCH
SNACK
DINNER

SHOPPING LIST
- ○ _____
- ○ _____
- ○ _____
- ○ _____
- ○ _____
- ○ _____
- ○ _____

NOTE

CARDIAC DIET MEAL JOURNAL PLANNER

WEEK _____   **MONTH** _____

MONDAY
BREAKFAST
LUNCH
SNACK
DINNER

TUESDAY
BREAKFAST
LUNCH
SNACK
DINNER

WEDNESDAY
BREAKFAST
LUNCH
SNACK
DINNER

THURSDAY
BREAKFAST
LUNCH
SNACK
DINNER

FRIDAY
BREAKFAST
LUNCH
SNACK
DINNER

SATURDAY
BREAKFAST
LUNCH
SNACK
DINNER

SUNDAY
BREAKFAST
LUNCH
SNACK
DINNER

SHOPPING LIST
- ○ _____
- ○ _____
- ○ _____
- ○ _____
- ○ _____
- ○ _____
- ○ _____

NOTE

CARDIAC DIET MEAL JOURNAL PLANNER

WEEK _____   MONTH _____

MONDAY

BREAKFAST
LUNCH
SNACK
DINNER

TUESDAY

BREAKFAST
LUNCH
SNACK
DINNER

WEDNESDAY

BREAKFAST
LUNCH
SNACK
DINNER

THURSDAY

BREAKFAST
LUNCH
SNACK
DINNER

FRIDAY

BREAKFAST
LUNCH
SNACK
DINNER

SATURDAY

BREAKFAST
LUNCH
SNACK
DINNER

SUNDAY

BREAKFAST
LUNCH
SNACK
DINNER

SHOPPING LIST

○ _____
○ _____
○ _____
○ _____
○ _____
○ _____
○ _____

NOTE

CARDIAC DIET MEAL JOURNAL PLANNER

 **Weekly**

WEEK _____   MONTH _____

MONDAY
BREAKFAST
LUNCH
SNACK
DINNER

TUESDAY
BREAKFAST
LUNCH
SNACK
DINNER

WEDNESDAY
BREAKFAST
LUNCH
SNACK
DINNER

THURSDAY
BREAKFAST
LUNCH
SNACK
DINNER

FRIDAY
BREAKFAST
LUNCH
SNACK
DINNER

SATURDAY
BREAKFAST
LUNCH
SNACK
DINNER

SUNDAY
BREAKFAST
LUNCH
SNACK
DINNER

SHOPPING LIST
- ○ _____
- ○ _____
- ○ _____
- ○ _____
- ○ _____
- ○ _____
- ○ _____

NOTE

CARDIAC DIET MEAL JOURNAL PLANNER

WEEK _____   MONTH _____

MONDAY
BREAKFAST
LUNCH
SNACK
DINNER

TUESDAY
BREAKFAST
LUNCH
SNACK
DINNER

WEDNESDAY
BREAKFAST
LUNCH
SNACK
DINNER

THURSDAY
BREAKFAST
LUNCH
SNACK
DINNER

FRIDAY
BREAKFAST
LUNCH
SNACK
DINNER

SATURDAY
BREAKFAST
LUNCH
SNACK
DINNER

SUNDAY
BREAKFAST
LUNCH
SNACK
DINNER

SHOPPING LIST
- ○ _____
- ○ _____
- ○ _____
- ○ _____
- ○ _____
- ○ _____
- ○ _____

NOTE

CARDIAC DIET MEAL JOURNAL PLANNER

WEEK _____   MONTH _____

MONDAY
BREAKFAST
LUNCH
SNACK
DINNER

TUESDAY
BREAKFAST
LUNCH
SNACK
DINNER

WEDNESDAY
BREAKFAST
LUNCH
SNACK
DINNER

THURSDAY
BREAKFAST
LUNCH
SNACK
DINNER

FRIDAY
BREAKFAST
LUNCH
SNACK
DINNER

SATURDAY
BREAKFAST
LUNCH
SNACK
DINNER

SUNDAY
BREAKFAST
LUNCH
SNACK
DINNER

SHOPPING LIST
- ○ _____
- ○ _____
- ○ _____
- ○ _____
- ○ _____
- ○ _____
- ○ _____

NOTE

CARDIAC DIET MEAL JOURNAL PLANNER

WEEK _____   MONTH _____

MONDAY
BREAKFAST
LUNCH
SNACK
DINNER

TUESDAY
BREAKFAST
LUNCH
SNACK
DINNER

WEDNESDAY
BREAKFAST
LUNCH
SNACK
DINNER

THURSDAY
BREAKFAST
LUNCH
SNACK
DINNER

FRIDAY
BREAKFAST
LUNCH
SNACK
DINNER

SATURDAY
BREAKFAST
LUNCH
SNACK
DINNER

SUNDAY
BREAKFAST
LUNCH
SNACK
DINNER

SHOPPING LIST
- ○ _____
- ○ _____
- ○ _____
- ○ _____
- ○ _____
- ○ _____
- ○ _____

NOTE

CARDIAC DIET
MEAL JOURNAL
PLANNER

WEEK _____   MONTH _____

MONDAY
BREAKFAST
LUNCH
SNACK
DINNER

TUESDAY
BREAKFAST
LUNCH
SNACK
DINNER

WEDNESDAY
BREAKFAST
LUNCH
SNACK
DINNER

THURSDAY
BREAKFAST
LUNCH
SNACK
DINNER

FRIDAY
BREAKFAST
LUNCH
SNACK
DINNER

SATURDAY
BREAKFAST
LUNCH
SNACK
DINNER

SUNDAY
BREAKFAST
LUNCH
SNACK
DINNER

SHOPPING LIST
- ○ _____
- ○ _____
- ○ _____
- ○ _____
- ○ _____
- ○ _____
- ○ _____

NOTE

CARDIAC DIET MEAL JOURNAL PLANNER

WEEK _____ MONTH _____

MONDAY
BREAKFAST
LUNCH
SNACK
DINNER

TUESDAY
BREAKFAST
LUNCH
SNACK
DINNER

WEDNESDAY
BREAKFAST
LUNCH
SNACK
DINNER

THURSDAY
BREAKFAST
LUNCH
SNACK
DINNER

FRIDAY
BREAKFAST
LUNCH
SNACK
DINNER

SATURDAY
BREAKFAST
LUNCH
SNACK
DINNER

SUNDAY
BREAKFAST
LUNCH
SNACK
DINNER

SHOPPING LIST
- ○ _____
- ○ _____
- ○ _____
- ○ _____
- ○ _____
- ○ _____
- ○ _____

NOTE

CARDIAC DIET MEAL JOURNAL PLANNER

WEEK _____   MONTH _____

MONDAY
BREAKFAST
LUNCH
SNACK
DINNER

TUESDAY
BREAKFAST
LUNCH
SNACK
DINNER

WEDNESDAY
BREAKFAST
LUNCH
SNACK
DINNER

THURSDAY
BREAKFAST
LUNCH
SNACK
DINNER

FRIDAY
BREAKFAST
LUNCH
SNACK
DINNER

SATURDAY
BREAKFAST
LUNCH
SNACK
DINNER

SUNDAY
BREAKFAST
LUNCH
SNACK
DINNER

SHOPPING LIST
- _____
- _____
- _____
- _____
- _____
- _____
- _____

NOTE

CARDIAC DIET MEAL JOURNAL PLANNER

WEEK _____   MONTH _____

MONDAY

BREAKFAST

LUNCH

SNACK

DINNER

TUESDAY

BREAKFAST

LUNCH

SNACK

DINNER

WEDNESDAY

BREAKFAST

LUNCH

SNACK

DINNER

THURSDAY

BREAKFAST

LUNCH

SNACK

DINNER

FRIDAY

BREAKFAST

LUNCH

SNACK

DINNER

SATURDAY

BREAKFAST

LUNCH

SNACK

DINNER

SUNDAY

BREAKFAST

LUNCH

SNACK

DINNER

SHOPPING LIST

- _____
- _____
- _____
- _____
- _____
- _____
- _____

NOTE

CARDIAC DIET MEAL JOURNAL PLANNER

WEEK _____   MONTH _____

MONDAY

BREAKFAST

LUNCH

SNACK

DINNER

TUESDAY

BREAKFAST

LUNCH

SNACK

DINNER

WEDNESDAY

BREAKFAST

LUNCH

SNACK

DINNER

THURSDAY

BREAKFAST

LUNCH

SNACK

DINNER

FRIDAY

BREAKFAST

LUNCH

SNACK

DINNER

SATURDAY

BREAKFAST

LUNCH

SNACK

DINNER

SUNDAY

BREAKFAST

LUNCH

SNACK

DINNER

SHOPPING LIST

- ◯ _____
- ◯ _____
- ◯ _____
- ◯ _____
- ◯ _____
- ◯ _____
- ◯ _____

NOTE

CARDIAC DIET MEAL JOURNAL PLANNER

WEEK _____   MONTH _____

MONDAY
BREAKFAST
LUNCH
SNACK
DINNER

TUESDAY
BREAKFAST
LUNCH
SNACK
DINNER

WEDNESDAY
BREAKFAST
LUNCH
SNACK
DINNER

THURSDAY
BREAKFAST
LUNCH
SNACK
DINNER

FRIDAY
BREAKFAST
LUNCH
SNACK
DINNER

SATURDAY
BREAKFAST
LUNCH
SNACK
DINNER

SUNDAY
BREAKFAST
LUNCH
SNACK
DINNER

SHOPPING LIST
- ○ _____
- ○ _____
- ○ _____
- ○ _____
- ○ _____
- ○ _____
- ○ _____

NOTE

CARDIAC DIET MEAL JOURNAL PLANNER

WEEK _____   MONTH _____

MONDAY
BREAKFAST
LUNCH
SNACK
DINNER

TUESDAY
BREAKFAST
LUNCH
SNACK
DINNER

WEDNESDAY
BREAKFAST
LUNCH
SNACK
DINNER

THURSDAY
BREAKFAST
LUNCH
SNACK
DINNER

FRIDAY
BREAKFAST
LUNCH
SNACK
DINNER

SATURDAY
BREAKFAST
LUNCH
SNACK
DINNER

SUNDAY
BREAKFAST
LUNCH
SNACK
DINNER

SHOPPING LIST
- ○ _____
- ○ _____
- ○ _____
- ○ _____
- ○ _____
- ○ _____
- ○ _____

NOTE

Made in the USA
Middletown, DE
28 February 2025

71989915R00061